Accidental Fruit

ACCIDENTAL FRUIT

CAROLYN OULTON

worple press

First published in 2016 by
Worple Press
Achill Sound, 2b Dry Hill Road
Tonbridge
Kent TN9 1LX.
www.worplepress.co.uk

Cover image by Carolyn Oulton
Author image by Paul Campbell

Printed by imprintdigital
Upton Pyne, Exeter
www.imprintdigital.com

Typeset and cover design by narrator typesetters and designers
www.narrator.me.uk
info@narrator.me.uk
033 022 300 39

ISBN: 978-1-905208-35-7

Acknowledgements

Thanks are due to the editors of the following publications, where some of these poems first appeared: *Ariadne's Thread*, *Elbow Room*, *Envoi*, *Ink, Sweat and Tears*, *Lunar Poetry*, *Seventh Quarry*, *Soul Feathers* (Indigo Dreams anthology), *Structo*, *Upstreet*.

Contents

Stories of the War

This is spring. Cut hedgerows
full of fingers, the sharp green
flicker of tiny branches
and up above the valley,
sudden hail.

       We thought we might see you.
      Who are you?

These are not my stories.
Her father was interred.
He can't remember when he fell.
She keeps the Golden Treasury.
He wishes he were dead.

       I'm Carolyn. I come to read.
      That would be nice.

He hasn't gone too far yet.
She keeps tickets in a book.
He's far from home.
Her mother always crying.
In his school there was a shelter.

      I have to go
      now. Goodbye.

These are not my stories.
This is spring.

Service Users' Book Club

I start again. *I wonder,*
why does he want so much
to go down to the sea?
 You play golf. You play by the sea.
And I wonder too – the ship,
What kind would it be?
 But no. You can't bring a ship
 up on to a golf course.

Later, raking out the sea
with my fingers:
a man remembers
Bristol and his father's voice,
a woman wants a doll's house,
the ex-eye surgeon finds me
patronising. A ship is running
down the flat for all it's worth.

Aurora Leigh in the Care Home

There is June. Born in December.
Mother had a sense of humour.
Janet, who won't tell me so,
Gwen, Carolyn (come to read), Audrey,
Sylvia – I not knowing there are three,
appropriate them all – and both the Peggys.

The wind has been up all night
punching pockets in the sky.
In this pub there are taps
and tea on draught,
disgraceful stories in the news,
a print of Churchill, sheaves of hops.

We've got Aurora safely through the house.
We sew, sew, prick our fingers, dull our sight,
Producing what? Sylvia wasn't brought up
to ask questions – *curse that stool!*
– or say what she was thinking.
She's waited a long time to laugh like this.

Waking to the light

Where are you.
By the sea,
across the shadow
where the rocks
climb out of water,
where the waves
turn to granite.

And where are you.
Through the gate
into the sun,
the smaller stones,
where a child is
straightening flowers,
speaking of death.

Home Movie

I can see the faces twice
through and above
the square inch of glass.
I start talking to it,
remembering myself.

Of course they don't hear
the hoarseness of hand on bark,
the flaying of blunt, uneven
flesh. Woodpecker faces
jabber from the mouth of an old tree.

A child in a hollow tree
waving or not waving?
where a man is standing
by a hollow tree
watching the face of a child.

Plane Passing

And suddenly the sky is ripped,
fired white while birds are cluttering
in deep-leaved branches;
dandelion clocks
clustering and bobbing,
suddenly airborne,
engines of summer.

Everything is moving
only a little,
under blue;
the sturdier branches
not even rippling when the sky
tears white, rips and fuzzes
and closes again.

Lines in a Victorian diary, January 1862 – August 2010

Monday morning. The computer ticks.
Yesterday he positioned me in stone,
dug holes in the sand;
we picked our way
down shingle to the sea.

Dig far enough and the sand
is alive with water.
A crush of flint, a scramble,
where the gathering waves
hesitate over pebbles.

Monday morning.

Words shape on a screen,
I'm sputtering footnotes:
croup, an illness of childhood,
23 he's been ill for days,
and 26.

He wants to know
where blood goes after death,
tries to interest his brother
in the Bible. His brother is two.
It doesn't work.

Monday morning letters turn to stone.

Forecast

The clouds that are least like snow,
rubbed by the shadow of a tree,
choking themselves – there, just
nearer than they were.
They are sure to bring it.

Whistle and the air
comes sticky like mint.
The wings of birds
slice like blades.
What happened was this.

Was how we waited,
the spire of the church
coming nearer, shabby clouds
marooned, stonewashed,
grinding blocks of snow.

New Year Suddenly

Now after rain, the electric
guzzle of a saw
ransacks branches, rough edged clouds
are saggy, gulls can't leave
that field alone, shuttlecock
corner to corner, snagging threads,
take the corners too fast.
Conifers fuss in too many layers,
the school gates sway and mutter,
ready for spring, about ready for spring,
where the air is shattering
blue in a hundred thousand directions at once.

School Run

An inch behind my shoulder
you'd changed your mind.
Your child could play with my child
but you had to come too.
We trundled into the wind,
your pushchair a recalculation
of biscuits (this was the child
who actually did
get hit by my child later on).

I shunted into the kitchen
two children of mine, plus one
anticipated for days, one additional
and you. Who had wanted to know
I wasn't some nutter –
we couldn't really get much
conversational mileage out of that.
So we sat and translated toddler.
He's saying dark. He's saying door.

Lines stolen from my daughter

The sky at lunch is strewn
with fish tails of cloud
rumpled in heaps.

All afternoon we slide
down the throats of trees
and sticky-tongued sunsets.

She's right. The moon is like
a banana – and before she sees
me looking, it's more like…

Accidental Fruit

In the middle of not something else
a child's moon is stuck
unwrapped on a fence.

Just before we're no longer
friends next door cocktails of flame
drench the chimney brick in mango and plum.

Morning is brisk with spring, ticking across
the splodgy cream of sunspill
kicked all over a flat-faced sky.

Threading the breeze

How to write all over the wind,
words dripping like boats
trailing foam;
and a toddler fixes his feet
in line with the shore,
threading family members in order.
Regularly spaced they call his name –
one voice alone hovers over the distance
We're going without you...

All night, the open window
tapping the door frame,
I was thinking of the downs,
fields prim with nettles,
the *leave this gate as you found it*
to the woods, where bird song
scatters, the wobble tongued bluebells
open their throats in the shade.
Leaves fan and flap against the air.

Travelling Backwards

Right she said. That's enough beauty
for today. I'm sitting now
in a station waiting room, crisp
and crunchy proper coffee freshly made.
Twenty minutes till my train

yesterday's rain falls
on the soft sacs of our eyelids,
closed where the wind
rummaged in among meadow grass.
What do you see? *The sea. The sea.*

Can you spot the difference between these two pictures?

Very blonde. The man writes down *vb*,
and behind us the sea is arching.
Bright pink top. *Pink top.*
Waves slither and slip.
Long shorts, blue and white

slip, slither and slide.
Nail varnish. Good thinking, Melissa.
Bright pink nails. That makes him
Conspicuous, surely. Why
do the waves start to lurch and chuckle?

Blonde. Pink top and blue / white shorts.
The man starts walking. *That's all we can do.*

The lines of the sea crumple and fold,
shiver and fall in, and then we find him
in the minutes before
it can start getting serious, playing
in a bright pink top with bright pink fingernails.

Wind Stripped

That evening we watched the wind
sweating the sky, the rain ran
sideways like beads on an abacus.

Times like that, wind breaks its back
shovelling the sea, grinding its teeth,
saws off edges of foam.

Afterwards the trees nod,
you're left with a clump
of leaves yanked off

in the night,
can't take your eyes
off the spot where they were.

A Walk in September

It wasn't, if I wanted to
remember it afterwards, that kind of wind,
breaking itself on fences,
sliding along flint
marking the fields.

I'd say that it gobbled
and gnawed its way
along overstrung branches,
tumbled in among the apples
chucking up leaves,

lolloped through fields,
jostled and rolled in green
and purple, bent trees at the hip,
scampered round houses
if it had been that kind of wind.

Glee

Just as in the song she'd
take out the ironing
to get at the cupboard
to open the dishwasher
unload the racks
go back to the table
to pick up the plates
to clear off the crumbs
bin the crusts, move
the marmite
play gogos

So the words fall down
all over it, the crying child
who won't wait.
The sea is watching
with hooded eyes,
a shout that is also
a cake, a splodge
of cream, a shaking
of crumbs.
Catching my legs, wanting
me now.

I ought to be working but

first I want to tidy up
that cupcake sun
at the top of the picture,
the dusty clouds;
bat at the light where it comes
drizzling and dribbling,
dives on to the sticky tips
of waves. Have both my hands
dipping like gulls
pecking at a keyboard
over a front of glass
like sugar frost.

@theVictorianheroine

If Victorian women had only
had access to email
and if shortly
after this – you're with me so far?
– everyday people such
as stalkers, disgruntled exes,
vaguely irritating neighbours
were then able to recover
the deleted text of emails,
three things would happen

to Victorian heroines:
land themselves in it
by email and be at the mercy
of disgruntled exes,
get talked over by the neighbours.

Under these conditions
a neighbour could have
their 90 minute quota but no more
to talk about what their children
had for lunch,
any given day
in the week of their choice.
After that I'd dub them in traceable emails
vapid as the heroine's blonde cousin
with her parents looking on.

This morning I loved

PETROL PANDEMONIUM!
The papers queue in racks
to where the sea is huffing
and clicking its jaws
again and again.

This morning I loved you
all over again by email
– *thanks for cleaning out
the chickens.* Traces of your pre-train
morning coffee in the sink.

The early morning bob
of bikes to school. Him off.
Did she think I was stuck
as you would have been, in mothers?
Taking my hand. *My mother, come on.*

Jerome K. Jerome in Walsall

'I seem to see and pity, going on before me, an innocent romantic boy, making his imaginative world out of such strange experiences and sordid things'.
David Copperfield

Yesterday I made it to your town.
Saw going on
before me the romantic child
dragged by us both
across pages just as a woman
walks to a chair
to act the part of a woman sitting.

The house itself
was self-conscious enough, and the street
half-heartedly Victorian. Just time
to beat the metre if I stuck
head and shoulders in the arcade
which I learn this morning
was after your time.

No man, you said, will ever
write the truth about his life.
If an interview by chance gets something right
you should be sure at once to strike this out.
Pain. *The Idler.* 1895.
I saw your house.
Nothing you knew was there.

Things I never did as a child

A proper apple pie. Done with a bolster.
Asterisk. Footnote. App. pie = bed.
Fagging. Being phased out. Plus my crush
didn't like me. Maybe here define term fag.
And crush. Add something here
about television closing down at six.
Lines. Not sure I did these. But board rubber
lobbing teacher obviously (Maths).
A jumble of odds and ends
time had finished with,
there where history ended.
I stumble around
those days every time
in the half-felt voice of a child.

Painting the Sea

A piano might just do it.
If it were possible of course
to get one out there
and if one knew
how to hit the notes
as if shoving and elbowing,
shouldering grit and
chucking it quite so untidily,
letting each note slide
into another
like small stones
bruising their backs
on water. Next the rasp
of bristles on paint.
This is a picture. In the picture
a small piano
is being eaten by the sea
while fragments
of what look like paper
smudge the outline,
bounce and hop against the frame.

Jumping Downs

With my head in position that butterfly wing
is the shadow of a line of grass –
just there the bone of a fallen thistle,
a boot hook. Coming up
the pink of my legs went cobweb,
an unnecessary detail.   This space is where
I wrote for fun with the point of a straw,
the brushing of the air a few inches up,
no ink or sound or colour for.
Those fields falling over themselves
are going to miss it, the touch
of a spider climbing my shoulder,
the red-tinged clover,
spilled tea shadows,
purple flowers as they tick tock tick.

Second prize answer
Hester C. Cholmondeley (aged 12 ¾)

They've digitised the journal I knew it was in,
the prize winning essay from 1882.
On birds. Attested by the governess
(the one from the missing diaries). At what age,
I wonder, does one stop
giving age as 'and ¾'?
If I'm truthful I was just
flicking before doing something else.
Hours afterwards I mean to write
about rain laid out in rows
along the backs of grass.
When I get the sudden pain.
Not so much the death at twenty two,
more the girl herself. I know
she wants to be a writer,
that her country house is beautiful,
that she and her sister both
like *Little Folks*. She writes
of the affectionate behaviour of caged birds.

The Watchers

Not the beach
laid out like sheet ice, waiting
for fractious waves
to ruffle along it, feet of dogs
to scuff and fracture it,
turn its sand the wrong way up
like lumps in gravy. Not the sea
itself, but the opening of curtains
on a tree, the puzzled faces
of two chickens staring in,
as I think what to say
about sand, and a sea
that stretches and wobbles its way
against it where it lies,
the texture of ice.

Cultural Studies

This is how it works.
The point at issue – let us say
that a woman to be good
must also be pure,
that one should raise one's hat to a lady,
that 5 ft 6 "should weigh
no more than eleven stone" –
the point is not,
in really effective writing,
ever quite stated but rather assumed.

The nurse, serenely tracking me down the page,
decoding and unravelling my forty years;
who measures and weighs (what she calls
the horrible bit), sets me personal goals,
dubs me moderately inactive
but only slightly overweight.
I tell her I love my body,
I tell her I happen
to have large breasts. *Just a few pounds
can make all the difference* she says.

Flowers in the Snow

Last week even the daffodils were confused
prodding the earth overhead.
And who can blame them, when the sea
keeps shaking itself
again and again at low tide
like badly-poured ale,
landing on heaps
of foam, tumbling off
spiky-headed rocks?

The moment the sun
jumps out from behind a wall,
sloshing in through the window,
lands in my mouth
and eyes and ears –
I lift my head that way,
as I will strain, old in my turn,
to listen. Just for a second
I thought it was spring.

Dry Ice

The fire might do better
if only I'd leave it alone.
I want to poke it to temper –
blow myself faint on the glow.

Close my eyes as the ash
flutters over my face.

After all it's a sulky sort of snow,
putting stodgy footsteps
on the air, can't quite
make up its mind for falling.

I wish I'd come out this morning
in my slippers to say goodbye.

Story on repeat

Every morning now
begins with snow
so that Nadia the white chicken
can get lost first.
Sandy, having red feathers,
goes down in a sunset.
Scarlet of course being black,
disappears in the dark.
When I need to clean my teeth
or run out of details,
they all come back to roost.

We've got the rhythm down –
and to this day…
But you know what happened,
don't you? If one morning
he said, *I should by now*?
When he first comes in
I'm awake to feel his footsteps;
seven and a minute
he's there on the bed.
Nadia story.
Everything was white…

Circus

Some mornings the sea
can't get out of bed,
skulks in ribbons of fat
chews its knuckles.
On days like this
it's crochet, needling shapes
of broken glass,
a stain on sand.
A circus, hooking an ankle
in strips of silk
to fall and twist and trace
its patterns in the shadow of the air.

Easter

Over Easter 2013 parts of the Dover coastline were eroded by severe weather, causing major chalk falls.

All night the sea listened.
Hour upon hour,
a hundred trumpets
lifted in the dark.

Chalk cartwheeling,
ammonites. By morning
the cliff is touched to the shape
and colour of a wing.

*If they were silent
the stones themselves would shout.*

The Web

A mosaic of threads,
something kicks and twists.
Under cover of the breeze
apples start to move stealthily
down branches, the voices of sheep
are deeper, the sky is full
of rocks, raindrops flick the skin
like minnows on a windowpane.

From the cliff

A hundred feet of falling
onto the back of the sea.
I watch it
rummage among bones
in rock pools and chalk.

Testing its strength,
a butterfly yanks its wings,
like the spotted pages
of a book too quickly opened,
breaking its stitches.

I wouldn't dare
to do it –
I know I'd fall
on those wings,
circling down like snow.

Channel Crossing

Stoned by the wind we stood
above a sea that kept chipping,
just as an egg skids and cracks in the boiling,
shell scaly, bursting out white.
Caught the sun a wash of colour sliding
down over the docks on the back of the moon.
I see it now as a child waves an arm in the mirror
as if for the very first time or as if for the last.

Hodnet, Shropshire. 1876

I fell through that footnote
like a face pressed too hard against glass.
I've seen the house you thought
you couldn't wait to leave,
talked over the descendants
of that cousin of yours with
the new curate. I'm glad
you got your London trip.
Strawberry cream ice, silk dress, new bonnets,
Kensington Museum and the underground.
The having to walk through the cold one night
for a cab. You guessed he was tipsy
(I'd call it London driving) but you wrote
in your diary later how you loved
the 'galop' and the streetlights,
how you had cleared out
your cupboard in the schoolroom
just before you left.

Phases of the Moon

Shadow on the bank like old washing,
trees mop headed, cloud bruising its hips
on cloud. All this I could have told you.
Down to the moon, heavy and replete,
bumping the sky. That it wasn't full
by a nick to the left, as metal
flicks along the contours of a fingernail.
No. It takes a seven year old
to notice something like that.

Toy Boats

From those few feet away
when the light comes tumbling,
losing its footing on the rocks,
and the sea like a ripped tea bag
shakes grit, the gulls
are buttoned on, watching the round
and roundness of children's play,
the string of ferries silent,
pulling along the other shore.

The Book

I liked the question. Yes,
I've been characters in books.
So when I was sitting
in that circle of readers,
I wasn't so much lying
or even joking
as simply showing off
in that aside
on my middle aged relations
with invisible friends.

I watched the nurse
unfold her arms and speak.
I heard the professor
cry for Sydney Carton, felt the child
testing adolescence on a paperback.
I was sitting in the vicarage garden,
its cucumbers and flowers,
as the dead writer rubbed
unheated walls for Newhaven,
for Hester, Rachel, Hugh.

Folkestone, New Year's Day

So no, I hadn't died then. Just been down
on the peppery beach, the other side
of the railings, where those last few crochet
poppies are being tattered in the wind.
I'd been watching my spit
twisting currents of air, the sea –
but this you knew already –
fold like broderie anglaise trimming the shore.
And salt-skimmed stitches
pulling my jaw to my cheek,
I found the stone I wanted, threw it
across my body. The great machine of the sea
rolling its shoulders, wound it in
like a spot of ink on a ribbon.
I turned and went back
to where you were coming towards me.
Oh hello. So you haven't died then?
Eyes like pebbles stretched in the wind.

Flood

A week ago outside my mother's house
an abandoned moon was facing our way,
sitting in a smooth, fat shadow
as if someone had suddenly bored
of colouring in.

The sky was hunched,
the rain kept coming,
Fields soggy as old towelling.

The road is a river, where engines
suck and throw out water in sparks
like Catherine Wheels. So excited.
I was so excited she said.
I was so excited I kept interrupting myself.

I knew it would start

on that morning,
if only because
the spiders' webs were flung
like hammocks across the grass,
each clearing the ground
by, say an inch;
dew springing back
along the wires.
I knew I'd begin it
on that morning,
standing in a field,
a voice calling
from the kitchen;
not really knowing
what would happen,
ankles wet with grass,
the morning light
mid-spring. That was how
I thought I could begin.

Before I am old

'And has the remnant of my life
Been pilfered of this sunny Spring?'
Dorothy Wordsworth

In the shadow of the woods
shapes push through like teeth,
bluebells hang steep,
bump against my tyres, through the field
the advance and retreat of a tractor.

I'm having that one for a start.
If I don't go through
those toys, who will? Read those PhD
chapters today, I'll never have time
to write comments before the review.

That's a second generation
of arthritis.
The toys are in the shed.
The work is done. If I can't get back
and look, I'm holding on to the wood and the cliff.

Word for emergency use

For HD

Oh death. You know how it is.
Never quite gets the message.
Like the child whose joke
you laughed at.
The holiday couple
who asked for your number.
You'll fall for it every time,
though it always
comes at the worst moment, right?
The one unutterably big
and inconvenient thing.

May in the Garden

I have kept faith with you, I hope.
N. will not be told
that she goes the wrong way about
pruning – I want to say begonia,
but being no great gardener myself…

Code for constant small adjustments,
diction of my youth. *I don't think we've met –*
less interrogation than polite command.
If you wonder how I know so much
about you, you're not giving it away.

A boy enters a room of faded yellow.
Candles, a stocking torn at the foot,
a shoe. The clocks have stopped.
I was warned about reading
in bad light. A myth, you say.

We remember being watched,
both of us, in other people's houses.
You read, I don't want you to stop.
But they did. The price (of being born a girl?)
of studying medicine at the time.

You tell me your aunts encouraged
your parents not to discourage it.
How you helped your father,
the Lewisham warden.
How your house was bombed.

So that was what you didn't
want to talk about last week.
He calls the knaves jacks. The cruelty.
You told me once, by the kitchen,
I needn't ask the driver to wait.

The clock moves in the garden.
I smile at Sylvia, sitting
in the shade. She sees me twice,
three times, among the daisies.
She won't talk to strangers though.

Early Work

Each desk has a width of, say, elbow to wrist.
Sanchez, who should be at one of them, isn't.
To pass the time, some of them get me
to take them to the lavatory. We invigilators
move among them, with self-important stealth.
Our fingers rock at our sides
or slide in to our pockets, as if
we were having our photo taken
and didn't know what to do with our hands.

1884.
Somewhere in an unscrubbed building
in Bloomsbury, a clerk wants to place
his life on the stage. Tries to avoid
desperation in letters to the editor.
Hasn't as yet bought the desk
which will later be held
by the birthplace museum, and later
still by the borough council.

1893.
Notable Women Authors of the Day
up and down the country, at keyhole desks
and charming oak bureaus, feel the
impossibility of a useful, domestic life,
recall their interrupted educations, shaky health,
keep up with letters – (my personal favourite)
*I could write novels as well as you
if I were not so weak in the wrist.*

Five minutes to go. At a hundred
Fully-stackable, wood-effect desks
pens wag like fingers.
History sweats in to the air.

Where the River Was

The pedal of my bike runs round
an inch above the stream
like the blade of an ice cream scoop,
curling skin off the water.

The soles of my feet taste it,
I'm guzzling mud
through cracks in the water,
shapes of upturned mushrooms

where the river runs down
through layers of silt,
to turn itself inside out again
somewhere under the earth.

Looking for a Sunset

When I rang to say I was ill,
I sounded so well
that just for a moment
I didn't believe myself.

How I can tell is by angles –
I have to keep
getting up and straightening things,
a hearth rug, a basket, a thought.

This memory of going out
in the evening in gum boots.
Being under the windows
and looking for a sunset.

Hundreds of leaves bend
as if held out on sticks. Shadows,
flint, and slapped on somewhere
near the bottom of the sky, a sun.

There, behind next door's trees,
stretched out along the grass, it must
have gone down. I next came across it
twitching in the early morning light.

Coming in to Fishbourne

If I could remember what you'd said
about that sea, I'd have it.
But for me, gulls' wings.
I still say, the wings of birds.
And the way that washing
flaps on a line.
The shape a child might make
biting a sandwich.
Quivering shadows
where a hand settles
for a moment on a sleeper's head.
Lizard skin. I said I would.
I'll keep it for you, then
we won't forget.

Heat-soaked

The butterflies themselves
are in a hurry
round the walls –
bricks sore with heat.
Down the lane the sheep need tuning,
the fluff of a dandelion clock
comes down like a plumb line.
Follicles splay
like my father's shaving brush
skimming the inches
between bone and bone,
fingers and face.
Somewhere in the trees a pigeon
is saying something over and over again.

After Rain

Up by Red Gate Shaw the long mud
trails like a crocodile.
I am not wearing blue,
open-toed sandals,
my mother, who in any case
avoids walks where possible,
is not bending near me, and this
is not Shottermill Pond or the 1970s
and I no longer have
the dress I may have been wearing,
but which in fact
I remember from a photograph.

Cow parsley is scorched,
dock seeds frizzle,
barbed wire rots on a fence.
My boot goes down as if
I were setting it in plaster.
I remember then
the foot of a child
jerking in mud.
And whether I comforted a child,
or was comforted, the trees
bend over me, water wriggles,
shaping cobwebs on the ground.

Incidental God

A wind bustles through branch
after branch, setting twigs
ticking as it shuffles
round leaves, a straw left
dangling from its mouth.

*This itself isn't prayer
but something near it –*

when a woman reaches
the corner of a building.
How a swing can
move along the stillness.
The shape of a shadow.

*This perhaps is prayer
or something like it –*

The stage spotted with light,
the characters tumbling
and not falling, the sight
of arms like wings, the glimmer
of the wires.

So this is prayer.
The wind's *Look at me* –

Help come just in time, physical
impossibilities and so forth.
In the end though it's more like
looking up just for a moment
and catching the wires.

Grass to the Head

A day later of course the butterfly was dead.
I'd shot it out of the house that afternoon.
In the evening I saw one like it
tense over a leaf. Ask me anything
about the rasp of its wings.
Or when, the next day,
a wasp got in among the washing.
Or even about the child and the nettle,
her leg in lumps like a jelly mould.
This I recall, was also
on the day after the butterfly died.

What I really want to know, is the word
that ran over my hair, a second
past that autumn grass just now.
I've long given up on why
some words smell of damp washing;
what it was I was thinking about,
when geraniums were first
a short cut to my grandmother
(these and the sound of pigeons).
All I know is where I was
the day after the butterfly died.

Creative Writing Induction

Then I pull on the ropes
and my lips begin to move.
I'm bound at this point
to beam at them all and confess
– there's no getting away from it –
This one is all about death.

No one could say it went
with the power point. Worse,
I had to stop smiling to read it,
while they in turn
had to try and care,
when we'd only just met.

The year we laid on sandwiches
(university policy then
being not to add any butter,
so I had to eat the lot),
literally the words
got stuck in my throat.

Death I'm ok with, can do.
It's understood, no one comes
an inch closer. It's more
the afterwards I mind.
Finding a chair.
The worry of meeting again.

Behind the Voices

Nearly a hundred years in black and white,
one by one they come bobbing
down the steps, speed as if time
itself or tape were running out.
Maisie, Muriel, Winifred and Claire.
Somewhere among them Tom, George
(killed in the next war), Harry,
Dorothy. A moment's pause,
then they do it all again
with husbands and wives,
Peggy with a trilby balanced
on what seems to be a mop.

My mother voices them over.
Just for a moment an older face
hovers on the screen,
says nothing, watches us
down the stone steps.

Then hours of rain,
a striped umbrella held
by a boy. A girl puts
a red ribbon to her hair.
A tapestry of trees shot
with green. Water
touches the sole of my foot.

Tidelines

In memory of Christopher Oulton 1959–2014

Afterwards the sea is sculpted
to the shape of dreams,
but the lines bulge and sag
in wrong places, shifting weight
over to an elbow, and slipping,
won't settle. Salt, unscrewed,
rushes with the shock of carbon
from a bottle. There is time
to kneel on the shingle and pray.
There is time to say
These people have seen me kneel
on the shingle and pray.
To turn and start the engine,
belt out a rhythm,
lose the signal on the radio,
re-thread the billion stitches of the sea.

Days After a Day

I work out that Wednesday is 13
because Tuesday is 14, on the day
when the wind
lies around untidily.
A window open in the bedroom,
weight of a blue curtain
soaked against the sill,
throw the door away from you
in the morning, stand
and gather the rain, kind of day.
Flowers in a vase
brittle as icing
by the afternoon, clouds
rot in the sky. Birds
rush through branches.
I turn back to the earth.

Notes for a Biography

I've lost a year at the start
and you missed out a death.
Mildly disloyal, I let that one go,
only too conscious already
of Mr K. on his PGCE placement.
I like the cloud formation
you've made of my life.
You ask me twice
is there anything to take out?
as if my birth or marriage
or knowledge of death
were too fragile a thing
to hold between this first page
and cover of your notebook,
prepared if you must
to throw your web of ink
over the letters and crack them.
Sifting at eleven
what is sometimes said
and what is left out.